"We watch the news, read articles, and hear stories about difficulties in our world. The needs are so massive, the stories so heartbreaking, that often we don't even know how to pray. Rachel Jones's excellent new book, *5 Things to Pray for Your World*, offers a needed guide to seek God's help by praying God's word. We may feel powerless, but we have the ear of an all-powerful God. May we faithfully cry out to him for the world around us."

Melissa Kruger, author, *The Envy of Eve* and *Walking with God in the Season of Motherhood*

"From Jesus' disciples to Martin Luther's barber and beyond, 'teach us to pray' has been a frequently heard heart-cry. *5 Things to Pray for Your World* will help you. It takes an old idea, tested and tried throughout the ages—a prayer list—and turns it into a thought-provoking, vision-expanding, prayer-stimulating tool. It is small enough to fit into your pocket, but big enough to change your life. Simple, but brilliant."

Dr Sinclair B. Ferguson, Ligonier teaching fellow and Professor of Systema
Westminster Theolog

"We all know we should pray for tl
where to start? *5 Things to Pray for*
a great option. It will expand the h
prayers as well as shaping them by (

Tim Chester, Pastor o
Boroughbridge, faculty memb
Training, and author of Y(

THINGS TO
5
PRAY

FOR YOUR
WORLD

RACHEL JONES

SERIES EDITOR: CARL LAFERTON

the**good**book
COMPANY

5 things to pray for your world
Prayers that change things for your community,
your nation and the wider world
© The Good Book Company, 2017
Series Editor: Carl Laferton

Published by
The Good Book Company
Tel (UK): 0333 123 0880
Tel (North America): (1) 866 244 2165
International: +44 (0) 208 942 0880
Email (UK): info@thegoodbook.co.uk
Email (North America): info@thegoodbook.com

Websites
UK & Europe: www.thegoodbook.co.uk
North America: www.thegoodbook.com
Australia: www.thegoodbook.com.au
New Zealand: www.thegoodbook.co.nz

ISBN: 9781784982584 | Printed in the UK

Design by André Parker

CONTENTS

PRAYING FOR YOUR WORLD...

SERIES INTRODUCTION

I wonder if you have ever struggled to believe this famous verse from the Bible?

> *"The prayer of a righteous person is powerful and effective." (James 5 v 16)*

James is telling us that when righteous people pray righteous prayers, things happen. Things change. The prayers of God's people are powerful. But they are not powerful because we are powerful, or because the words we say are somehow magic, but because the Person we pray to is infinitely, unimaginably powerful. And our prayers are effective—not because we are special, or because there is a special formula to use, but because the God we pray to delights to answer our prayers and change the world because of them.

So what is the secret of effective prayer—how can you pray prayers that really change things? James suggests two questions that we need to ask ourselves.

First, are you righteous? A righteous person is some-one who is in right relationship with God—someone who, through faith in Jesus, has been forgiven and accepted as a child of God. Are you someone who, as you pray, is praying not just to your Maker, not just to your Ruler, but to your heavenly Father, who has completely forgiven you through Jesus?

Second, do your prayers reflect that relationship? If we know God is our Maker, our Ruler and our Father, we will want to pray prayers that please him, that reflect his desires, that line up with his priorities for our lives and for the world. The kind of prayer that truly changes things is the prayer offered by a child of God that reflects God's heart.

That's why, when God's children pray in the Bible, we so often find them using the word of God to guide their prayers. So when Jonah prayed in the belly of a fish to thank God for rescuing him (Jonah 2 v 1-9), he used the words of several psalms strung together. When the first Christians gathered in Jerusalem to pray, they used the themes of Psalm 2 to guide their praise and their requests (Acts 4 v 24-30). And when Paul prayed that his friends would grow in love (Philippians 1 v 9), he was asking the Father to work in them the same thing the Lord Jesus prayed for us (John 17 v 25-26), and which the Holy Spirit is doing for all believers (Romans 5 v 5). They all used God's words to guide their words to God.

How can you pray prayers that are powerful and effective—that change things, that make things happen? First, by being a child of God. Second, by praying Bible prayers, which use God's words to make sure your prayers are pleasing to him and share his priorities.

That's what this little book is here to help you with. It will guide you on how to pray for the world—both close to home and further afield—in 21 different areas and situations. In a sense, each page is an extension of what our Lord taught us to pray: "Your will be done, on earth as it is in heaven" (Matthew 6 v 10). God's will is that this be a world that reflects his character—a world of love, truth, justice and, most of all, ever-increasing worship of his Son. Each prayer suggestion is based on a passage of the Bible, so you can be certain that they are prayers that God wants you to pray for his world.

There are five different things to pray for each of the 21 areas. So you can use this book in a variety of ways.

- You can pray a set of "five things" each day, over the course of three weeks, and then start again.

- You can take one of the prayer themes and pray a part of it every day from Monday to Friday.

- Or you can dip in and out of it, as and when you want and need to pray for a particular aspect of the world around you.

- There's also a space on each page for you to write in the names of specific people, organisations or places that you intend to remember in prayer.

This is by no means an exhaustive guide—there are plenty more things that you can be praying for this world! But you can be confident as you use it that you are praying great prayers—prayers that God wants you to pray. And God promises that "the prayer of a righteous person is powerful and effective". That's a promise that is worth grasping hold of confidently. As we pray trusting this promise, it will change how we pray and what we expect to come from our prayers.

When righteous people pray righteous prayers, things happen. Things change. So as you use this book to guide your prayers, be excited, be expectant, and keep your eyes open for God to do "immeasurably more than all we ask or imagine" (Ephesians 3 v 20). He's powerful; and so your prayers are too.

Carl Laferton
Editorial Director
The Good Book Company

YOUR COMMUNITY

YOUR CHURCH IN THE COMMUNITY

2 THESSALONIANS 3 v 1-5

PEOPLE TO PRAY FOR:

_____

_____

_____

_____

Father, please grant...

 ## HONOUR FOR CHRIST

"Pray for us that the message of the Lord may spread rapidly and be honoured, just as it was with you" (v 1).

Thank God for all the people in your church family who have honoured Christ by submitting their lives to him. Pray that the message of Jesus would spread rapidly in your community, as more and more people honour Christ as their Lord and Saviour too.

 ## PROTECTION

"Pray that we may be delivered from wicked and evil people, for not everyone has faith" (v 2).

If a church is not facing any opposition from the community, it's sometimes because they're not taking risks with the truth. So ask God to make you bold. Pray for special protection for your church leaders as they minister in risky situations and proclaim unpopular truths.

3 OBEDIENCE

> *"We have confidence in the Lord that you are doing and will continue to do the things we command" (v 4).*

Ask God to help your church family to be obedient to all that he commands in his word—at work and at home, in public and in private, in what you say and what you do. Pray that your distinctive lives would be a powerful witness to those around you.

4 LOVE

> *"May the Lord direct your hearts into God's love…" (v 5).*

Thank God for his deep, unfathomable love for you. Pray that this love would overflow in the way your church family treats one another—so that as a lonely world looks on, they see something attractively countercultural. Ask God to make you better at embracing newcomers and outsiders with this love too.

5 PERSEVERANCE

> *"… and Christ's perseverance" (v 5).*

As the years and decades go by, pray that you would not grow weary in seeking to share Christ with your friends and neighbours. Pray for specific people you know who have come into the orbit of the church and heard the gospel, but have remained indifferent or drifted away. Ask God to help you persevere in your witness to them.

3 DO GOOD

"Live such good lives among the pagans…"
(v 12).

Prayerfully think through some practical ways you can pro-actively do good to your neighbours this week. Ask for God's help to show genuine interest, radical hospitality and real love to those living around you.

4 EXPECT ACCUSATION

"Though they accuse you of doing wrong…"
(v 12).

If we live and speak wholeheartedly for Jesus, we can expect to meet some opposition—no matter how "nice" we are. Ask God to give you an attitude which expects and embraces this, so that you won't shy away from broaching awkward conversations or giving invitations to church.

5 GLORIFY GOD

Ask that your neighbours would "see your good deeds and glorify God on the day he visits us" (v 12).

On the day that Jesus returns, every single person on your street will bow the knee to him. But pray that your neighbours would do that now, willingly—so that on that day they will meet Jesus as their Saviour as well as their Judge. Take time to pray this for some of your neighbours by name.

YOUR COMMUNITY

A LOCAL
SCHOOL

PROVERBS 1 v 1-7

SCHOOLS TO PRAY FOR:

_____

_____

_____

_____

THANK GOD

Thank God that he has provided everything we need "for gaining wisdom and instruction; for understanding words of insight" in his word (v 1-2).

While human minds wonder at the puzzle of *how* the world around us works, God has not left us guessing on the question of *why*—he's told us clearly through Scripture. Thank God for that!

Then pray that God would make this school a place where students and teachers...

GET FUTURE-PROOFED

Pray that students would learn "prudent behaviour" (v 3).

Thank God for the way he uses education as an instrument of his common grace in restraining the effects of sin on society. Pray that this school would teach children "prudent behaviour", and equip them to make choices that do good, not harm, to others as they grow up.

3 LOVE FAIRNESS

Pray that students would learn to do "what is right and just and fair" in God's eyes (v 3).

Sometimes it seems that our culture's definition of right and wrong is drifting further and further from the Bible's definition. But pray that children in this school would be taught that what God thinks is right is indeed right; that what God says is just is indeed just; and that what God says is fair is indeed fair.

4 LEARN DISCRETION

Ask God to teach "discretion to the young" (v 4).

Kids can be very cruel with their words. So pray that these children would learn to control their tongues and speak words that are kind and patient, not offensive or mean.

5 FEAR GOD

"The fear of the LORD is the beginning of knowledge" (v 7).

Pray that students and teachers would come to fear God—and realise that this is far more important than all the knowledge the world offers. Pray for Christian teachers you know, and anyone else who has an opportunity to witness to the gospel—ask that they too would fear God, not humans, and so speak faithfully and courageously of Jesus.

YOUR COMMUNITY

LOCAL
WORKPLACES

GENESIS 1 v 27-29;
3 v 17-19

WORKPLACES TO PRAY FOR:

_____

_____

_____

_____

Pray that local businesses and places of work would…

 ## REFLECT GOD'S IMAGE

Thank God that he "created mankind in his own image" (1 v 27).

Thank God that this truth gives every person's work real dignity—when we work, we're reflecting the image of our Creator God, no matter how "menial" our job. Pray that staff at this workplace would come to embrace this truth.

 ## WORK TOGETHER

"Male and female he created them" (1 v 27).

Humans can do more together than we can do on our own—because that's the way God made us. And when we work together, we reflect something of our three-in-one God. So thank God for the many different people who work together in this place, and ask him to bless their working relationships. Pray that their different skills and experiences would come together in the grand task of ruling over God's created world—and all to his glory.

3 ENJOY PROSPERITY

"I give you every seed-bearing plant on the face of the whole earth and every tree that has fruit with seed in it" (v 29).

Thank God for the abundant provision of his creation—in the natural world he has provided all the raw materials that this business needs to flourish. Pray that he would graciously cause this business to prosper as people put God's gifts to work.

4 CARE FOR THE EARTH

"Rule over the fish in the sea and the birds in the sky and over every living creature that moves on the ground" (1 v 28).

God has given humankind the earth to use, but also to care for. Pray that this business would carry out its work in a way that protects and cares for other people and the environment.

5 LOOK TO THE SNAKE-CRUSHER

Pray for those who experience "painful toil" and face "thorns and thistles" (3 v 17-18).

Work is good—but because of sin, it's also frustrating. Thank God that the One he promised to send to "crush [the snake's] head" (v 15) and overturn the effects of sin has indeed come. Pray that those frustrated by work would understand why the world is not as it should be, and look to Christ, who will put all things right again when he returns.

YOUR COMMUNITY

HOSPITALS & EMERGENCY SERVICES

2 CORINTHIANS 1 v 3-11

PEOPLE AND PLACES TO PRAY FOR:

 PRAISE GOD

Praise God that he is "the Father of compassion and the God of all comfort, who comforts us in all our troubles" (v 3-4).

Think back to emergency situations or periods of ill-health when God has comforted you. Thank God that he stands ready to comfort all those who turn to him for help.

 COMFORT IN TROUBLE

"... so that we can comfort those in any trouble with the comfort we ourselves receive from God" (v 4).

Pray that Christian doctors, nurses, chaplains and patients would have opportunities to share something of their own faith with those in trouble. Ask God to help them speak of the only good news that can offer lasting comfort—that Christ can heal our relationship with God so that we can enjoy life to the full, for ever. Pray by name for any Christians you know personally.

3 RELIANCE ON GOD

> *"We felt we had received the sentence of death. But this happened that we might not rely on ourselves but on God, who raises the dead" (v 9).*

However good our healthcare is, only God is in control of life and death. Pray that both patients and professionals would come to appreciate their own helplessness in the face of death—and turn to rely on God, who raises the dead.

4 DELIVERANCE FROM DANGER

> *"He has delivered us from such a deadly peril, and he will deliver us again. On him we have set our hope that he will continue to deliver us..." (v 10).*

God loves to deliver people from danger, including ill-health—in his grace, he often works through the skill of doctors and nurses. Ask him to use these professionals to save many lives and restore people to full health.

5 ANSWERS TO PRAYER

> *"... as you help us by your prayers. Then many will give thanks on our behalf for the gracious favour granted us in answer to the prayers of many" (v 11).*

Give thanks for the way God has answered your prayers in the past. Who else can you "help by your prayers" right now?

YOUR COMMUNITY

THE POOR & MARGINALISED

ISAIAH 58 v 6-11

PEOPLE AND PLACES TO PRAY FOR:

_____

_____

_____

_____

Father, in your mercy please give...

 JUSTICE FOR THE OPPRESSED

"Loose the chains of injustice" (v 6).

Praise God that he is perfectly just—he cares passionately about those who are oppressed by low pay, unfair employment practices and ill-health. Pray that your church would be passionate about those things too. Ask God to show you how he would have you spend your money, cast your vote and give your time in order to "loose the chains of injustice".

 FOOD FOR THE HUNGRY

"Share your food with the hungry" (v 7).

Who is "hungry" in your community? And what would it look like to "share" your food with them, not just give your food to them? Often our paths just don't seem to cross with those of people in need—but ask God to give you eyes to see such people. Pray that he would open up a way for you to help them practically, while also reaching out in genuine friendship.

3 SHELTER FOR THE HOMELESS

"Provide the poor wanderer with shelter"
(v 7).

Pray for the homeless in your area; for the ones that are easy to see, because they live on the street, but also for those who are harder to see, because they live in temporary and unsuitable housing. Ask God to help the authorities and charities working to provide shelter for them.

4 RESPECT FOR THE POOR

"Do away with ... the pointing finger and malicious talk" (v 9).

Who is looked down on in your community? Is it the jobless, the "problem families", the addicts, those who speak a different language? Repent of any ways in which you yourself have "pointed your finger" at the poor. Ask God to help you honour the poor in the way you think and talk about them.

5 NEVER-FAILING WATERS

Pray that your church would be "like a well-watered garden, like a spring whose waters never fail" in your community (v 11).

Pray that your church family would be a distinctive, refreshing and beautiful presence in your area as you hold out the water of life to all who are thirsty. Ask that many lost people would be drawn to have the LORD as their "guide ... always" (v 11).

YOUR COMMUNITY

PRISONS

ACTS 16 v 25-40

PEOPLE AND PLACES TO PRAY FOR:

THANK GOD

Thank God for this truth: "Believe in the Lord Jesus, and you will be saved" (v 31).

It really is that simple! Thank God that salvation is available to anyone. No one's heart is too wicked, and no one's past is too tragic. No one's crimes are so bad that they cannot be covered by Christ's death on the cross, and no one's life is so messed up that it can't be transformed by the Holy Spirit.

Then pray for your nearest prison and ask God for...

BELIEVERS TO SPEAK

"Then they spoke the word of the Lord to him and to all the others in his house" (v 32).

Pray that God would provide many believers to speak the word of God in this place. Pray for the work of prison chaplains, and for Christian guards, visitors and inmates. Pray that each one would faithfully speak of Jesus to those around them.

HEARERS TO BELIEVE

"He was filled with joy because he had come to believe in God—he and his whole household" (v 34).

In the space of just seven verses the jailer goes from suicidal dread (v 27) to overflowing joy (v 34). Pray that many in this prison would experience a similar transformation as they hear and believe the gospel.

FAIR TREATMENT

"They beat us publicly without a trial, even though we are Roman citizens, and threw us into prison. And now do they want to get rid of us quietly? No! Let them come themselves and escort us out" (v 37).

Pray that justice would be done without prejudice, and that every person in this prison would be treated fairly and with dignity.

A LOVING CHURCH

"After Paul and Silas came out of the prison, they went to Lydia's house, where they met with the brothers and sisters and encouraged them" (v 40).

Pray that your church would be a place that embraces ex-offenders, even when they're not like Paul and Silas—ask God to give you grace to love the difficult people that society doesn't want to give a second chance to.

YOUR NATION

THE GOVERNMENT

1 TIMOTHY 2 v 1-6

POLITICIANS TO PRAY FOR:

_____

_____

_____

_____

 THANK GOD

> "I urge ... that ... thanksgiving be made for all people—for kings and all those in authority" (v 1-2).

The Bible "urges" us to give thanks for our rulers—so do that now! Good governments provide order, restrain wickedness, facilitate human cooperation and protect the vulnerable—and these are all things that God loves. So give thanks for specific ways in which your government is doing this. Ask God to make you more conscientious in offering "petitions, prayers [and] intercession" for your government too.

Pray that your government would allow...

 PEACE AND QUIET

> "... that we may live peaceful and quiet lives" (v 2).

Pray that God would use your government's policies to improve wellbeing and promote peace: peace between nations, peace between communities, and peace within families.

3 GODLINESS TO FLOURISH

Pray that the government would protect religious liberty and enable Christians to live "in all godliness and holiness" (v 2).

Pray that your government would give Christians the freedom to obey God's law and live as he tells us to. Pray about any specific ways that this is under threat.

4 KNOWLEDGE OF THE TRUTH

"This is good, and pleases God our Saviour, who wants all people to be saved and to come to a knowledge of the truth" (v 3-4).

Compared to the situation for Paul's first readers, your government may well give you considerable religious freedom already. So pray that the church would make good use of it! Pray that we wouldn't be content to live in cloistered comfort, but rather, would urgently be reaching out to those around us with "the truth" of the gospel, so that they might "be saved".

5 PRAISE GOD

Praise God that there is a "mediator between God and mankind, the man Christ Jesus, who gave himself as a ransom for all people" (v 5-6).

God has provided what "all people" in your nation need: a ransom. Pray by name for particular politicians—ask that they would see their need of a mediator and recognise Christ as the only way to be saved.

YOUR NATION

THE JUSTICE
SYSTEM

ROMANS 13 v 1-7

PEOPLE TO PRAY FOR:

_____

_____

_____

_____

 ## THANK GOD

"The authorities that exist have been established by God ... The one in authority is God's servant for your good" (v 1, 4).

Thank God for establishing the justice system in your nation. Thank him for lawmakers, the police force, courts, judges and juries, all of which he has established for "our good"—to restrain human evil and enable the flourishing of society.

Then pray that the authorities would...

 ## COMMEND GOOD

"Do what is right and you will be commended" (v 3).

Pray for those who make, interpret and enforce the law; that in doing so, they would commend what is truly "right" in God's eyes (even if they don't recognise that themselves). Pray too for Christians working in the police force and the legal system. Ask God to help them to "do what is right" in their day-to-day work.

PUNISH WRONGDOING

"They are God's servants, agents of wrath to bring punishment on the wrongdoer" (v 4).

Ask God to help the authorities in bringing wrongdoers to justice. Pray that the guilty would be caught, brought to trial, fairly tried, found guilty, and appropriately punished, because this is God's will.

RECEIVE DUE SUBMISSION

"It is necessary to submit to the authorities" (v 5).

Pray that people would keep the law! Not just with regard to major crimes ("not only because of possible punishment"), but also in the smaller offenses that are usually never found out ("but also as a matter of conscience"). Consider and confess to God the times when you have not submitted to the law.

BE RESPECTED

"Give to everyone what you owe them: ... if respect, then respect; if honour, then honour" (v 7).

Pray that the police and legal authorities would be held in respect by your culture—not necessarily because their conduct is always honourable, but because God has put them in a position of authority. Ask God to help you to give them respect and honour in your own heart too.

YOUR NATION

THE ARMED FORCES

PSALM 46

PEOPLE AND PLACES TO PRAY FOR:

_____

_____

_____

_____

Father, please help those in the military to...

 NOT FEAR

> *Thank God that he "is our refuge and strength, an ever-present help in trouble. Therefore we will not fear" (v 1-2).*

Ask God to help you not to be fearful about international security, or unduly anxious for the people you love. Ask God to give military personnel this same courage in the face of trouble—courage that comes from knowing the Ruler of the universe as their heavenly Father. Think too of the families who are waiting back home; pray that they would know God with them, helping them to entrust their fears to him.

 PRAISE GOD

> *"Nations are in uproar, kingdoms fall; he lifts his voice, the earth melts" (v 6).*

What nations are in uproar? Which regimes around the world are fighting to keep their grip on power? Praise God that he rules over all of these situations—his voice is powerful enough to make the earth melt.

3 ESTABLISH PEACE

"He makes wars cease to the ends of the earth" (v 9).

Where are your armed forces currently engaged? Cry out to God to bring this conflict to an end and establish peace in that region soon. Thank God that one day every tank, every missile and every piece of armour will be obsolete when he establishes his new creation.

4 KNOW GOD

"Be still, and know that I am God" (v 10).

Pray for the work of armed-forces chaplains, and for Christian military personnel and their families. Pray that in the busyness of service life, they would take time to hear from God in his word and enjoy his presence daily. Ask that through their patient witness, many more people in your armed forces would come to know that the LORD is God, and find their rest in him.

5 DISPLAY GOD'S GLORY

"I will be exalted among the nations, I will be exalted in the earth" (v 10).

In the moral complexities of international conflicts, it's often hard to know what to pray for, or what the best solution would be. At times like this, we can confidently and simply ask that God would be glorified: *God, may your name be exalted among the nations; God, may your name be exalted in the earth.*

YOUR NATION

THE MEDIA

ZECHARIAH 8 v 16-21

YOUR NATION

HUMAN
TRAFFICKING

PSALM 10

PEOPLE AND CHARITIES TO PRAY FOR:

_____

_____

_____

_____

 LORD, SEE THEM

> "[The wicked man] says to himself, 'God will never notice; he covers his face and never sees'" (v 11). Thank God that this is not true!

There are thousands of victims of human trafficking and slavery living in your country (and more than 20 million worldwide). Most of us don't know who they are or where they live, but thank God that _he_ does. God knows each victim by name and sees every perpetrator—and he cares, deeply.

2 LORD, STOP THEM

> "Arise, LORD! Lift up your hand, O God … Break the arm of the wicked man" (v 12, 15).

Ask God to intervene to stop the wicked actions of human traffickers. Pray that he would break their power and free many from slavery.

3 LORD, HELP THEM

"The victims commit themselves to you; you are the helper of the fatherless" (v 14).

Pray that those who are currently in slavery would cry out to God in their helplessness—and that he would help them. Pray for churches and Christian charities who are working with trafficking victims. Ask that through their work many vulnerable people would come to know God as their heavenly Father through Christ.

4 LORD, PUNISH THEM

"Call the evildoer to account for his wickedness that would not otherwise be found out" (v 15).

Ask God to use the police force and justice system to find, prosecute and punish traffickers. And rejoice that even when human judges fail, Christ will be a perfect judge—and one day, God will hold *all* evildoers to account for their actions.

5 LORD, COME BACK SOON

Rejoice that one day "mere earthly mortals will never again strike terror" (v 18).

Thank God that he has promised to make a new creation that is free from all pain and fear—pray that he would do that soon. Echo in your own heart the words of the apostle John: *"Amen. Come, Lord Jesus"* (Revelation 22 v 20).

YOUR NATION

CHILDREN
IN CARE

DEUTERONOMY 10 v 14-22

PEOPLE AND FAMILIES TO PRAY FOR:

_____

_____

_____

_____

Use this to pray for children and young people who are adopted, fostered, or in the care of social services.

1 CHOSEN

"To the LORD your God belong the heavens, even the highest heavens, the earth and everything in it. Yet the LORD set his affection on your ancestors and loved them, and he chose you" (v 14-15).

Praise God for that awesome truth! Thank him that "he chose you" and has adopted you as his child. Thank him for giving us human adoption as a picture of this extravagant divine adoption.

2 PROTECTED

"He defends the cause of the fatherless and the widow..." (v 18).

Thank God that he is on the side of those with no one to care for them. Pray that he would enable social services, the police and family courts to protect vulnerable children and fight for their interests.

3 LOVED

"… and loves the foreigner residing among you, giving them food and clothing. And you are to love those who are foreigners" (v 18-19).

God commands his people to look after the needy— so pray that more Christians would open their homes, hearts and wallets for the sake of needy children and teenagers. And ask God to show you how he wants *you* to live out his care for the vulnerable.

4 STEADFAST

"Fear the LORD your God and serve him. Hold fast to him" (v 20).

Pray for any Christians you know who are parenting fostered or adopted children. Pray that they would cling to God in all the challenges which that brings, seeking to serve him first and foremost, and submitting all their fears and worries to him in prayer.

5 GOD'S CHILDREN

"He is your God, who performed for you those great and awesome wonders you saw with your own eyes" (v 21).

Bring before God any fostered or adopted children you know. Ask him to open their eyes to understand his "great and awesome" salvation through Christ— so that one day they would enjoy the security of having the LORD as "their God" too.

YOUR NATION

PRAYING IN THE WAKE OF A TRAGEDY

JOHN 11 v 1-43

PEOPLE AND SITUATIONS TO PRAY FOR:

_____

_____

_____

_____

Some incidents can shake a whole nation with horror and grief. In those moments, pray that people would...

 CALL ON JESUS

"The sisters sent word to Jesus" (v 3).

In the face of the overwhelming tragedy of death, there is ultimately only one person we can turn to for help: Jesus. So call on him now. And pray that, as people around you are distressed and perplexed by tragedy, this would cause them to cry out to Jesus too.

 SEE GOD'S GLORY

"It is for God's glory so that God's Son may be glorified through it" (v 4).

Disasters often leave us asking, "Why, God?" But we know that God in his sovereignty weaves together all events to glorify his Son—even when, from a human perspective, that seems impossible. And God's glory is what matters most—so pray now that he would indeed be glorified, even as you rejoice in the knowledge that he definitely will be.

3 RECEIVE ETERNAL LIFE

"I am the resurrection and the life. The one who believes in me will live, even though they die; and whoever lives by believing in me will never die" (v 25-26).

Thank Jesus for this promise. Thank him that his resurrection guarantees your resurrection. Pray for some of the people affected by this tragedy—ask that they would come to "believe in [Jesus]", so that one day they "will live, even though they die".

4 KNOW THAT JESUS CARES

"When Jesus saw her weeping ... he was deeply moved in spirit and troubled ... Jesus wept" (v 33, 35).

Thank Jesus that he knows how it feels to cry with grief. Pray that those closely affected by this tragedy would come to see Jesus as we see him in this story—deeply grieved for the hurting, and outraged at the intrusion of suffering into his creation. Ask God to give you a more compassionate—more Christ-like—heart.

5 WITNESS GOD'S INTERVENTION

"The dead man came out" (v 43).

Just as the Father accepted his Son's prayer (v 41-42), so he accepts the prayers of his Son's people. So what might it look like for God to intervene in this situation for good? (Don't think too small, because our God is not small!) Then ask him to do that thing now.

5 THINGS TO PRAY

YOUR WORLD

A PLACE AFFECTED BY

WAR OR TERROR

PSALM 56

PLACES AND PEOPLE TO PRAY FOR:

_____

_____

_____

_____

Bring a place affected by war or terror before God and pray...

 ## FOR THOSE UNDER ATTACK

"Be merciful to me, my God, for my enemies are in hot pursuit; all day long they press their attack" (v 1).

Pray for those people whose lives are in danger right now—perhaps in the line of fire, or critically ill in hospital. Ask God to show mercy to them and protect them.

 ## FOR THE FEARFUL

"When I am afraid, I put my trust in you" (v 3).

When we see stories of war and terror in the news, we feel vulnerable. Pray for some specific people you know who are afraid of a world that seems out of control—ask that this sense of helplessness would drive them to the LORD, who is in control. Thank God that when we're trusting in Christ, we do not need to fear death; we can say confidently with David, "What can mere mortals do to me?" (v 4).

FOR THE WICKED

> *"Because of their wickedness do not let them escape; in your anger, God, bring the nations down"* (v 7).

Ask God to use the authorities or international community to bring the perpetrators to justice. Thank him that no wickedness will ultimately go unpunished, since one day everyone will face his perfect justice.

 FOR THE GRIEVING

> *"Record my misery; list my tears on your scroll—are they not in your record?"* (v 8).

Thank God that he hears the cries of those who are mourning—not one tear shed will be forgotten or unaccounted for in God's faultless reckoning of the world on judgment day. Ask him to comfort the grieving in their misery, especially with this promise.

 FOR SURVIVORS

> *"You have delivered me from death and my feet from stumbling, that I may walk before God in the light of life"* (v 13).

News reports from war zones always bring reports of casualties—but they almost always bring stories of survivors too. So thank God for those he has delivered from physical death. Ask God to extend his spiritual rescue to them too—that they would come to see Jesus as the light of the world, and spend the rest of their life walking with him.

YOUR WORLD

A PLACE AFFECTED BY

NATURAL DISASTER

1 KINGS 8 v 37-43

PLACES AND PEOPLE TO PRAY FOR:

_____

_____

_____

_____

 THANK GOD

> *"Whatever disease or disaster may come, and when a prayer or plea is made by anyone among your people ... then hear from heaven" (v 37-39).*

Solomon prayed this prayer at the opening of the Jerusalem Temple. But when Christians pray, we have even greater grounds for confidence than Solomon—because we approach God not through an animal sacrifice, but on the basis of his Son's perfect sacrifice. So we know for certain that our heavenly Father hears us. Praise God for that wonderful privilege!

2 FORGIVE

> *Ask God to "forgive" (v 39).*

Natural events often only become "natural disasters" because of human greed, corruption and selfishness—and it's usually the most vulnerable who suffer the consequences. Cry out to God for forgiveness for when this has been the case. Pray that he would mercifully spare people from the consequences of human sin.

ACT

Ask God to "act" in this situation to save many from harm (v 39).

Pray for the work of disaster-relief agencies—ask God to empower their efforts to help those in need. Pray too for governments seeking to respond to this crisis— ask God to help them make wise decisions.

4 SHOW EXTRAVAGANT GRACE

"As for the foreigner who does not belong to your people ... when they come and pray towards this temple, then hear from heaven ... Do whatever the foreigner asks of you..." (v 41-43).

Whatever people's religion or lack of one, disasters often cause them to turn to the divine for help. And although God doesn't owe anyone an answer, his character is gracious and merciful. Pray that those caught up in this disaster would somehow turn to the true God for help; and that, in his love, God would answer the pleas of the desperate.

 MAKE HIS NAME KNOWN

"... so that all the peoples of the earth may know your name and fear you" (v 43).

Ask God to grow the church in this nation. Pray that in the wake of this disaster, more and more people would come to truly know God—fully and finally re-vealed in the person of Christ.

YOUR WORLD

A PLACE UNREACHED BY THE GOSPEL

ROMANS 10 v 1, 9-15

PLACES AND PEOPLE TO PRAY FOR:

_____

_____

_____

_____

Use this to pray for unreached people—whether in another country or living closer to you.

 PRAYERFUL PEOPLE

> *"Brothers and sisters, my heart's desire and prayer to God for the Israelites is that they may be saved" (v 1).*

Repent of the ways in which you lack Paul's concern for the lost. Ask God to make it your "heart's desire and prayer" that these people would be saved—that as you pray for them now, the Spirit would mould your heart to make it more compassionate, like Christ's. Ask God to help you to persevere in prayer on their behalf.

 THANK GOD

> *Thank God that he "richly blesses all who call on him ... 'Everyone who calls on the name of the Lord will be saved'" (v 12-13).*

God is not stingy with his saving grace; he is over-whelmingly generous. Thank God that he intends to bring people of every nation, including this one, into relationship with him.

3 DECLARE AND BELIEVE

Pray that people in this nation would "declare with [their] mouth, 'Jesus is Lord,' and believe in [their] heart that God raised him from the dead" (v 9).

Ask God to establish his church in this part of the world.

4 SEND SOMEONE TO PREACH

"How can they hear without someone preaching to them?" (v 14).

Pray for any believers you know who are already seeking to share the gospel here. Ask God to make them faithful—clearly communicating the unchanging truth of God's word; and ask him to make them flexible—doing so in way that resonates with this particular culture. Ask God to raise up many more men and women willing to renounce self-interest and embrace risk in order to preach the good news in this area.

5 PROMPT CHURCHES TO SEND

"And how can anyone preach unless they are sent?" (v 15).

Pray that your church would be a generous sending church, ready to give money and let go of people in order to reach the unreached. Ask God to even send someone from your church to this particular community! Then pray for other churches around the world—that they too would answer the call to send workers to this place.

YOUR WORLD

A PLACE WHERE CHRISTIANS ARE PERSECUTED

2 CORINTHIANS 4 v 7-15

PLACES AND PEOPLE TO PRAY FOR:

_____

_____

_____

_____

Father, help Christians in this country to...

 ## DISPLAY GOD'S POWER

> *"We have this treasure in jars of clay to show that this all-surpassing power is from God and not from us" (v 7).*

Thank God for the "treasure" of the gospel: "the knowledge of God's glory displayed in the face of Christ" (v 6). Thank God for how, throughout history, he's always used weak people to take his gospel forward. Pray that although the church in this nation looks weak by human standards, God would work through them to put his all-surpassing power on display.

 ## NOT DESPAIR

> *"We are hard pressed on every side, but not crushed; perplexed, but not in despair" (v 8).*

Do you know of particular believers who are especially "hard pressed" at this time? Pray for them now. Ask God to encourage them by his word today, so that they would hold on to hope and "not ... despair".

BE PROTECTED

> *"Persecuted, but not abandoned; struck down, but not destroyed" (v 9).*

Pray that these Christians would remember that they are "not abandoned"—they do not face their persecutors alone, but have Christ's own Spirit dwelling in them. And ask God to protect this church—that although it is being "struck down", he would prevent it from ever being completely destroyed.

SPEAK BOLDLY

> *"We also believe and therefore speak" (v 13).*

Pray that believers in this country would speak of their faith to others, even when that puts them in danger. Ask God to fill them with the same confidence as Paul had in the face of death: "… because we know that the one who raised the Lord Jesus from the dead will also raise us" (v 14).

REACH MORE WITH GRACE

> *"All this is for your benefit, so that the grace that is reaching more and more people may cause thanksgiving to overflow to the glory of God" (v 15).*

Pray that more and more people in this country would experience the joy of God's saving grace. One day in eternity you will be standing side by side with believers from this nation, thanking and glorifying Jesus—and you can start doing that now.

YOUR WORLD

A POST-
CHRISTIAN
COUNTRY

1 CORINTHIANS 1 v 18 – 2 v 5

PLACES AND PEOPLE TO PRAY FOR:

Pray that a nation rejecting its Christian past will have:

CONFIDENCE IN THE CROSS

"The message of the cross is foolishness to those who are perishing, but to us who are being saved it is the power of God" (v 18).

Thank God that he has provided a way to crush the power of sin and death: the cross of Christ. Ask God to give his people real confidence in this message—even when the Bible's values are ridiculed by their culture. But the message of the cross can and will save, so pray that Christians in this nation would proclaim that message fearlessly.

DOUBT IN HUMAN WISDOM

"I will destroy the wisdom of the wise; the intelligence of the intelligent I will frustrate" (v 19).

"There is no such thing as absolute truth"; "If it feels right it must be right"; "What you can see is all there is". Ask God to show people the futility of their worldviews, so that they would see this worldly "wisdom" for what it really is: lies.

HUMILITY BEFORE GOD

"God chose the weak things of the world to shame the strong ... so that no one may boast before him" (v 27-29).

Pray that God's people in this nation would have a genuine sense of their own weakness, so that they have a healthy humility before him. Pray that this would make them more prayerfully reliant on him.

REDEMPTION THROUGH CHRIST

Praise God for this truth: "It is because of [God] that you are in Christ Jesus, who has become for us wisdom from God—that is, our righteousness, holiness and redemption" (v 30).

Ask God to redeem many people from this nation, making them right with him through Christ Jesus. Pray by name for particular people you know.

A WORK OF GOD'S SPIRIT

"My message and my preaching were not with wise and persuasive words, but with a demonstration of the Spirit's power" (2 v 4).

Thank God that his work is not reliant on our skill! Pray that the church in this country would never be duped into thinking that what they most need is a slicker sales pitch—they need the Spirit's power. So ask God to do a great work by his Spirit in this nation.

5 THINGS TO PRAY

YOUR WORLD

A RELIGIOUS
COUNTRY

ACTS 14 v 8-23

PLACES AND PEOPLE TO PRAY FOR:

_____

_____

_____

_____

Pray for a country that is religious, but not Christian…

FOR TORN CLOTHES

"When the apostles Barnabas and Paul heard of this, they tore their clothes and rushed out into the crowd" (v 14).

When the people of Lystra tried to worship Paul and Barnabas, the apostles were so grieved that they tore their clothes. And the thought of millions of people practising a false religion, perhaps without ever even hearing the name of Jesus, should deeply grieve us too. Ask God to press this upon your heart. Pray that, like Paul and Barnabas, you'd be driven to an urgent response right now: prayer.

FOR GOOD NEWS

"We are bringing you good news" (v 15).

Thank God for the gospel, that we can be forgiven and accepted by God through the death and resurrection of Christ Jesus. Ask God to raise up more messengers of this good news, so that many people would "turn from … worthless things to the living God".

3 FOR GOD'S TESTIMONY

"He has not left himself without testimony"
(v 17).

Thank God for "showing kindness" to the people of this nation by giving them food, and "filling their hearts with joy". What grace! Pray that this testimony would point people to the God of grace. Thank God for also giving us a testimony that is even clearer still: the story of Jesus in the words of the Bible. Pray that many would read and respond to it.

4 FOR ENDURANCE IN HARDSHIP

"We must go through many hardships to enter the kingdom of God" (v 21-22).

What hardships might Christians in this nation be facing? Pray that these disciples would be strengthened and encouraged in the face of hardship (v 21), as they keep their eyes fixed on the eternal kingdom of God (v 22).

5 FOR A HEALTHY CHURCH

"Paul and Barnabas appointed elders for them in each church and, with prayer and fasting, committed them to the Lord" (v 23).

Ask God to establish his church in this place—a whole network of healthy, thriving congregations. Pray that their elders would be faithful and godly shepherds. Perhaps you know of a particular church or pastor; commit them to the Lord by name.

YOUR WORLD

A MISSIONARY

2 TIMOTHY 1 v 7-13

PLACES AND PEOPLE TO PRAY FOR:

_____

_____

_____

_____

Father, help this missionary to...

 LOVE POWERFULLY

> *"For the Spirit God gave us does not make us timid, but gives us power, love and self-discipline" (v 7).*

Spirit-fuelled love is not "timid" in putting itself out for others, but is willing to take a risk to love like Jesus in word and deed. So ask God to fill this missionary with radical love: love for local believers, love for team-mates, and love for those who are lost without Christ.

 SUFFER WELL

> *"Join with me in suffering for the gospel, by the power of God" (v 8).*

What sort of suffering might be wearing this missionary down? Ill-health? Hostility? Loneliness? Pray that God's powerful Spirit would help them to endure. Ask God to reassure them that his gospel really is worth suffering for. (And maybe you could be the answer to your own prayer by the power of email or letter...)

3 BE HOLY

"He has saved us and called us to a holy life" (v 9).

Thank God for saving this missionary and calling them to follow Jesus. Pray that they would grow in holiness as they fight against sin.

4 REMEMBER GRACE

Thank God that "he has saved us ... not because of anything we have done but because of his own purpose and grace. This grace was given us in Christ Jesus before the beginning of time" (v 9).

God's work is all of grace: pray that this truth would keep this missionary from pride when things are going well, and keep them from discouragement when things are going badly.

5 TEACH FAITHFULLY

"What you heard from me, keep as the pattern of sound teaching, with faith and love in Christ Jesus" (v 13).

Ask God to protect his church from false teaching. Pray that this missionary would set an example of "sound teaching" that is faithfully taught, wisely applied, and focused on Christ Jesus. Where, when and to whom does this missionary teach the Bible? Pray for those occasions now.

ALSO AVAILABLE IN THE RANGE:

BEST RESOURCE 2017

THE EDEN
WINNER
1
AWARDS

We all want to pray and know it's important, but our prayer lives can get stuck in a rut.

These books will give you lots of ideas when you don't know what to pray. Each page takes a passage of Scripture and suggests 5 things to pray for a friend or family member, or an area of church life. Because when we pray in line with God's priorities as found in his word, our prayers are powerful—they really change things.

THEGOODBOOK.CO.UK/5THINGS

thegoodbook
COMPANY

BIBLICAL | RELEVANT | ACCESSIBLE

At The Good Book Company, we are dedicated to helping Christians and local churches grow. We believe that God's growth process always starts with hearing clearly what he has said to us through his timeless word—the Bible.

Ever since we opened our doors in 1991, we have been striving to produce resources that honour God in the way the Bible is used. We have grown to become an international provider of user-friendly resources to the Christian community, with believers of all backgrounds and denominations using our Bible studies, books, evangelistic resources, DVD-based courses and training events.

We want to equip ordinary Christians to live for Christ day by day, and churches to grow in their knowledge of God, their love for one another, and the effectiveness of their outreach.

Call us for a discussion of your needs or visit one of our local websites for more information on the resources and services we provide.

Your friends at The Good Book Company

UK & EUROPE   thegoodbook.co.uk   0333 123 0880
NORTH AMERICA   thegoodbook.com   866 244 2165
AUSTRALIA   thegoodbook.com.au   (02) 9564 3555
NEW ZEALAND   thegoodbook.co.nz   (+64) 3 3343 2463

 WWW.CHRISTIANITYEXPLORED.ORG
Our partner site is a great place for those exploring the Christian faith, with a clear explanation of the good news, powerful testimonies and answers to difficult questions.